San Diego
CALIFORNIA

A PHOTOGRAPHIC PORTRAIT

PHOTOGRAPHY BY

STEVE GOULD

NARRATIVE BY

SARA DAY

TWIN LIGHTS PUBLISHERS | ROCKPORT, MASSACHUSETTS

Copyright © 2015 by
Twin Lights Publishers, Inc.

All rights reserved. No part of this book may be reproduced in any form without written permission of the copyright owners. All images in this book have been reproduced with the knowledge and prior consent of the artists concerned and no responsibility is accepted by producer, publisher, or printer for any infringement of copyright or otherwise, arising from the contents of this publication. Every effort has been made to ensure that credits accurately comply with information supplied.

First published in the United States of America by:

Twin Lights Publishers, Inc.
Rockport, Massachusetts 01966
Telephone: (978) 546-7398
www.twinlightspub.com

ISBN: 978-1-934907-38-2

10 9 8 7 6 5 4 3 2 1

(opposite)
Torrey Pines State Reserve and State Beach

(frontispiece)
San Diego Skyline from Shelter Island

(jacket front)
San Diego Evening Skyline from
Coronado Island

(jacket back)
San Diego Harbor and
Unconditional Surrender Sculpture

Major League Baseball trademarks and copyrights are used with permission of Major League Baseball Properties, Inc.

Special thanks to SeaWorld and Hotel Del Coronado who have kindly consented to appear in this publication.

Many thanks to Wendye Conn for her knowledge and guidance.

Book design by:
SYP Design & Production, Inc.
www.sypdesign.com

Printed in China

America's Finest City

Overlooking the vast Pacific Ocean from a vantage point of massive sculpted cliffs painted gold by a setting sun, one cannot help but absorb the stunning beauty of the San Diego coastline. This ethereal vision is a fitting invitation to discover much more about the multi-layered culture, intriguing history, and fascinating people that make this place "America's Finest City."

The City of San Diego was shaped culturally by both Native American and Spanish influences well before it became part of the United States in 1848, after the Mexican-American War. With the first mission established in the state by Father Junipero Serra in 1769, San Diego would become known as the "birthplace of California." Today, it is the eighth largest city in the United States, contributing much to the region through a booming economy fueled by innovative entrepreneurship, a prominent U.S. military presence, international trade, and a tourism industry that invites millions of visitors to explore its fascinating history and alluring natural beauty.

From Balboa Park to La Jolla, from the Sorrento Valley to Mid-City, there's a certain energetic vibe that permeates through the city's thriving culinary, art, musical, and theatrical scene. San Diego was host to both the Panama-California Exposition in 1915 - 1916 and the California Pacific International Exposition in 1935 - 1936, and continues to be a center for international events including invitational tournaments held at Torrey Pines Golf Course and Comic-Con that draws tens of thousands of comics and sci-fi fans each year.

San Diego is a city of historic adobe structures and modern architecture. Dynamic and ever-changing, it is a unique blend of past and present—all the while with a curious and spirited pulse on the future. Crisp and clean; bold and vibrant—these are words that best describe both the imagery from the lens of talented photographer Steve Gould and the incredible city he has so beautifully captured.

House of Hospitality
BALBOA PARK *(opposite)*

Architect Carleton M. Winslow designed the Foreign Arts Building for the 1915 – 1916 Panama-California Exposition. Also known as the House of Hospitality, the Spanish Renaissance-style building was demolished and replicated in 1997 in order to better withstand an earthquake.

Oceanside Pier at Twilight
OCEANSIDE

Lights sparkle along Oceanside Pier and cast a warm glow on the calm surface of the Pacific Ocean. Built in 1987, the 1,954-foot-long wooden pier is one of six that had previously succumbed to storms. At the end of this popular fishing spot is Ruby's Diner where they're always serving up delicious classic American cuisine.

Oceanside Harbor
OCEANSIDE

Charter, commercial fishing, sailing and more, busy Oceanside Harbor boasts 900 permanent slips. This quaint harbor hosts some 200,000 visitors a year, many of whom spend time strolling through the many boutiques and restaurants of the seaside main-street-of-old called Harbor Village.

Oceanside Beach
OCEANSIDE *(top)*

Oceanside Beach boasts 3.5 miles of sandy shores, rolling surf, and outstanding ocean views. The relaxing seaside retreat features Oceanside Pier, where locals and visitors often gather to enjoy great music, grab a bite to eat, cast a line, or simply enjoy a long, leisurely stroll by the sea.

World Bodysurfing Championship
OCEANSIDE *(bottom)*

With a surf that averages a fun and consistent 3.5 to 4 feet, it's clear why Oceanside Beach hosts the World Bodysurfing Championship each year. Some 400 bodysurfers, ranging in age from 12 to over 65, travel far and wide to ride the cresting waves during the popular, two-day event.

Old Mission San Luis Rey de Francia
OCEANSIDE *(above and right)*

Padre Fermin Francisco de Lasuen founded Old Mission San Luis Rey de Francia in 1798. Home to Franciscan Friars, it is the largest of 21 California missions and has been fittingly dubbed the "King of the Missions." The mission is a National Historic Landmark and is open to the public.

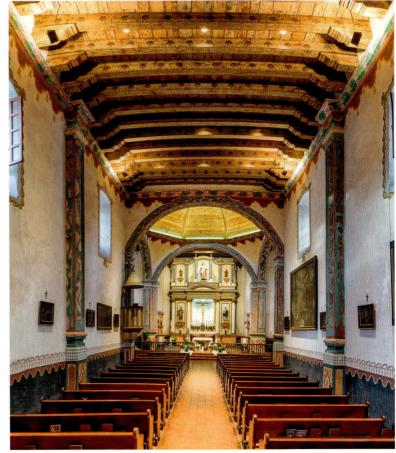

Legoland®

CARLSBAD (top)

One of six located worldwide, Legoland California Resort is an interactive themepark where the beloved building-block toys come to life. Kids of all ages can enjoy a waterpark and an aquarium, as well as rides and attractions such as *Land of Adventure, Miniland USA,* and *Imagination Zone.*

Miniland USA

CARLSBAD (bottom)

Made entirely of Lego building blocks, a jaw-dropping replica of downtown San Francisco is one of seven different U.S. sites that comprise Miniland USA, in Legoland. With amazing detail, including popular landmarks and moving buses, the combined sites use 20 million building bricks in 1:20 scale.

The Flower Fields at Carlsbad Ranch
CARLSBAD

Awash in a sea of botanical beauty, visitors stroll among 50 acres of multi-colored Giant Tecolote Ranunculus blooms. The Flower Fields burst into a proverbial rainbow of color for six to eight weeks each spring. A popular venue for special occasions, the ranch also hosts concerts, flower shows, and a photography workshop.

Nature's Mirror
ENCINITAS *(top)*

The magnificent cliffs located north of Moonlight Beach are mirrored in tide pools along the shore, revealing nature's splendor in varied tones of flaxen light. The golden hour entices visitors to experience the drama of San Diego's waterfront topography in glorious detail.

Vintage Woodie
ENCINITAS *(bottom)*

Hip and eclectic, Encinitas is a surf-side city of boutique shops, great restaurants, meditation gardens, yoga studios, and vintage cars from a by-gone era. Having several glorious beaches from which to choose along South Coast Highway 101, Encinitas is a surfer's heaven with a distinct 1960s vibe.

Swami's Beach

ENCINITAS

The bluffs at Sea Cliff Park are a relaxing vantage point with spectacular views of Swami's Beach, a prime spot sought out both locally and internationally for its excellent surfing conditions. The beach is named for Swami Paramahansa Yogananda, founder of the Self-Realization Fellowship ashram located here.

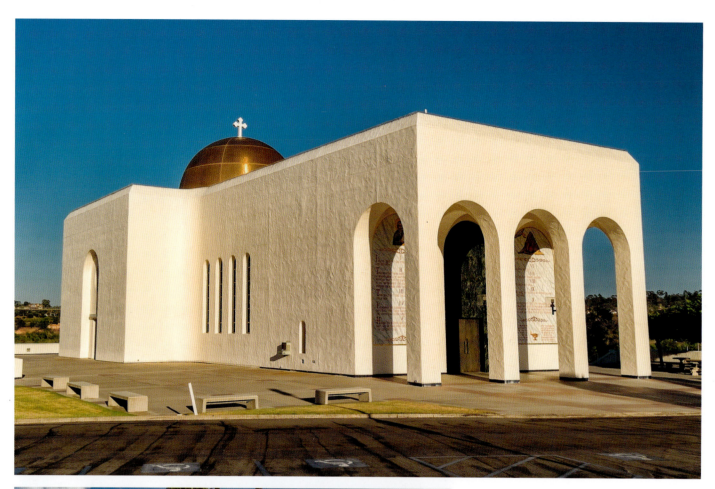

Saints Constantine and Helen Greek Orthodox Church
CARDIFF-BY-THE-SEA *(above)*

Simple and beautiful, from architectural design to interior iconography, the Saints Constantine and Helen Greek Orthodox Church on Manchester Avenue was consecrated in 2001. It is also known as the "Church of the Shining Cross" as the sun reflects the shape of a cross on its golden dome daily.

Self-Realization Fellowship
ENCINITAS *(left and opposite)*

The Self-Realization Fellowship ashram was founded in 1920 by spiritual guru, Paramahansa Yogananda. The residing order reaches out to the community offering yoga, lectures, meditation, retreats, and spiritual counsel guided by the teachings of their world-renowned founder.

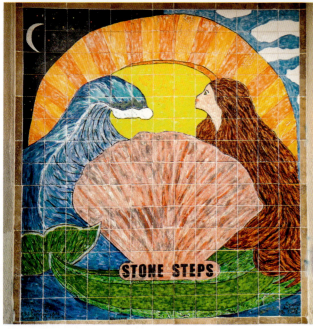

Stone Steps Beach
ENCINITAS *(left)*

Nearly 100 concrete steps descend from the top of the bluff to the beach below. Located between Moonlight State Beach and Beacons Beach, it is one of Encinitas more secluded spots. Since the land is totally covered here at high tide, visitors must enjoy their sandy stroll only when the tide is low.

San Diego Botanic Garden

ENCINITAS *(above and opposite top)*

From subtropical fruits to desert succulents, the San Diego Botanic Garden is a paradise one can explore year-round. The grounds include 27 different gardens spanning 37 acres, including the Hamilton's Children Garden. The garden also offers tours, educational programs, bird watching, and special events.

Bernardo Winery
RANCHO BERNARDO *(top and bottom)*

Founded in 1889, Beranrdo Winery is the oldest operating winery in the state. The winery not only bottles some of the finest regional vintages, but also includes the Village Shops, where you'll find delectable foods, jewelry and clay artisans, specialty boutique, a salon, yoga studio, and dance theatre.

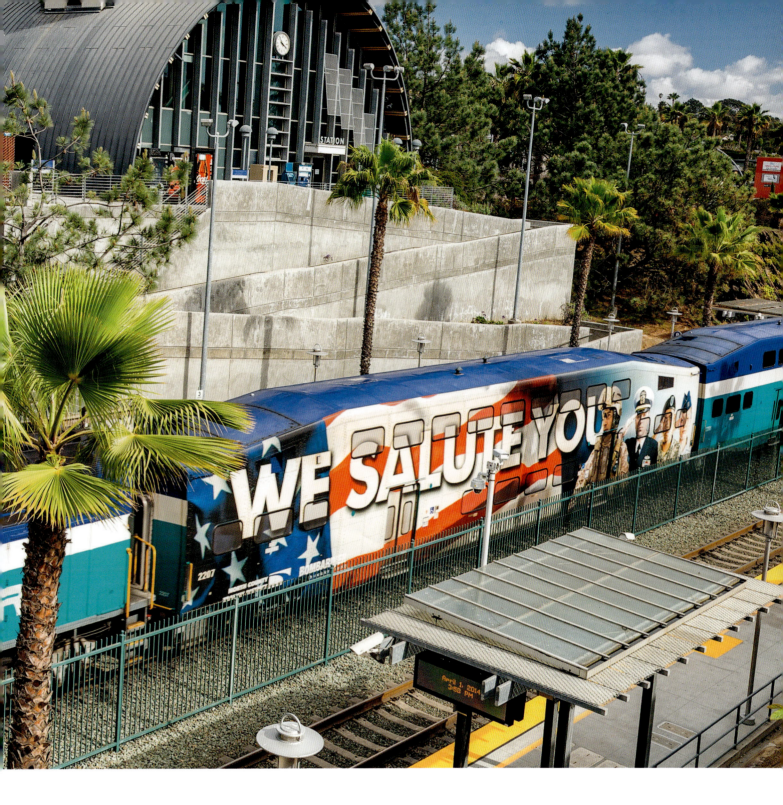

Solana Beach Train Station
SOLANA BEACH

The busy Solana Beach station services over 1,000 people per day along the Amtrak California's Pacific Surfliner and North County Transit District's COASTER commuter rail routes. The station's modern, semi-circular building was designed in 1994 by architect Rob Wellington Quigley.

Surfing
DEL MAR *(top)*

An avid surfer challenges the crest of a near-perfect wave. Del Mar Beach is known for its legendary surf, with consistent swells and reef breaks year-round. Del Mar has been included in *Time* magazine's list of the "100 Greatest Beaches in the World."

Powerhouse Park
DEL MAR *(bottom)*

In 1928, a powerhouse was built at this site to supply heat and hot water to a hotel and cottages. Today, the historic building serves a community center within Powerhouse Park. The park is a long stretch of green space where visitors can enjoy the beautiful seashore, summer concerts, and nearby waterfront dining.

Del Mar Beach
DEL MAR *(opposite)*

The setting sun dips into the horizon as a brilliant amber sky paints a dramatic end to another perfect day. With unique and diverse wave areas at the north, middle, and south, Del Mar Beach provides some of the best surfing conditions in Southern California.

Del Mar Fairgrounds
DEL MAR *(above)*

The Del Mar Fairgrounds encompass nearly 340 acres, and includes 180,000 square feet of exhibit space. It hosts nearly 350 agricultural and entertainment events each year including the popular San Diego County Fair.

San Diego Polo Club
RANCHO SANTA FE *(left)*

Located in Rancho Santa Fe, the San Diego Polo Club is 60-acres of thundering equine excitement. The world-class facility was founded in 1986 and includes five polo fields, riding trails, a training school, exercise track, and clubhouse. Sunday Polo is open to the public from May to October.

Del Mar Thoroughbred Club
DEL MAR *(above and right)*

Located at the Del Mar Fairgrounds, this world-class American thoroughbred race track opened in 1937. Opening day features the famous hat contest and the season continues with exciting horse racing from July through September, Friday-night concerts, and Family Fun Day on Saturdays and Sundays.

Surf Dog
DEL MAR *(top)*

Dogs rule the tide as this poised pup proves. In a color-coordinated blaze of foam and fur, it's clear from this pooch's sly grin, that pets can most certainly get just as much fun out of water sports than their human counterparts.

Dog Beach
DEL MAR *(bottom)*

Furry friends convene for an afternoon of energetic romping at Dog Beach, located at the mouth of the San Dieguito River. Whether engaging in a "tug-of-war" or chasing a tennis ball, friendly canines and their owners would agree, this is an amazingly picturesque beach on which to spend the day.

San Diego County Fair
DEL MAR *(opposite)*

From festival foods to garden exhibits, from farm animals to exhilarating rides and challenging contests, the San Diego County Fair draws over one million people to this fun, 24-day festival each summer. Held at the Del Mar Fairgrounds, there's always something new to discover at the fair.

Grape Day Park
ESCONDIDO *(above)*

Designed by Nancy Moran and Valerie Salatino of Nature Works, Inc., *Vinehenge* is a super-sized public-art project where children play among giant sculptures and hidden secrets are waiting to be found. A historic landmark, Grape Day Park is Escondido's oldest park and was the center of the Grape Day Harvest celebration from 1908–1950.

Escondido Civic Center
ESCONDIDO *(left)*

The first phase of the Escondido Civic Center project, Escondido City Hall features a stunning, web-like gazebo over the courtyard. The award-winning design is part of a cultural center that includes a community theatre, performing arts theatre, art museum, as well as government offices.

Torrey Pines State Beach
TORREY PINES

Boogie boarders catch their last ride of the day as dusk casts pink and purple hues upon the ocean's surface. Torrey Pines State Beach stretches 4.5 miles from Del Mar to La Jolla. The Northern end of the beach is for surfers while the Southern end is reserved for swimmers and bodysurfers.

Cliffs at Torrey Pines

TORREY PINES

Zen-like panoramic ocean views can be seen from atop the plateau of massive sandstone cliffs that cascade to the beach below—on a clear day, to the north, Del Mar; to the south, La Jolla. These amazing cliffs are part of the Torrey Pines State Natural Reserve, one of the most scenic parks in the world.

Gliderport
LA JOLLA (above)

A common, yet alluring, site along the San Diego coast, paragliders, launched from atop the scenic cliffs, are effortlessly airborne—taking in the spectacular view from a fascinating vantage point. Torrey Pines Gliderport is a glider airport, owned by the city of San Diego and enjoyed by soaring enthusiasts for more than 80 years.

Evening Hot Air Balloon
CARMEL VALLEY (right)

For a different type of soaring experience, a hot air balloon ride is a terrific way to enjoy a birds-eye view of the Southern California coast. The natural beauty of San Diego's wine country and the awe inspiring Pacific coastline as seen from a tranquil 1,500 feet is an adventure not soon forgotten.

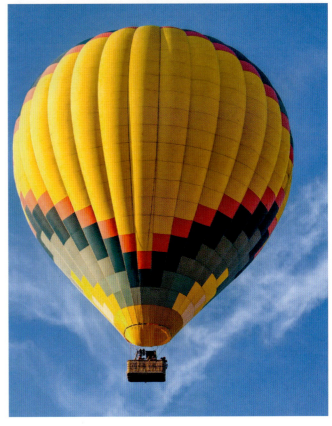

Torrey Pines State Beach
LA JOLLA

The colossal cliffs at Torrey Pines State Beach are reflected in the wet sands over which they loom at low tide. Beachgoers seem to walk on mirrored glass as they stroll along a golden image during low tide. One of several hiking trails in the area, the 3/4-mile Beach Trail leads visitors to the sandy shore below.

Vibrant Skies

LA JOLLA *(top)*

Whether gazing from the cliffs above or beach below, the sunset along the San Diego coastline is nothing short of magical. Vibrant hues of magenta and orange blend with soft violets and reflect onto the surface of the incoming tide as if answering an encore to another perfect Southern California day.

Surf Fishing

LA JOLLA *(bottom)*

Anglers cast into the bountiful waters of the San Diego coastline—well known for its exceptional surf fishing. Enthusiasts can catch dinner from a long list of species that vary from season to season, such as surfperch, corbina, rockfish, white sea bass, sheephead, croaker, and halibut.

Torrey Pines Golf Course

LA JOLLA *(above and left)*

Stunning ocean views are par for the course at the award-winning Torrey Pines Golf Course—one of the country's top municipal golf courses. Home to professional tournaments such as the U.S. Open, it opened in 1957 and includes two 18-hole courses designed by renowned course architect, William P. Bell.

Torrey Pines State Reserve

LA JOLLA (above)

Massive cliffs cascading to the beach below are part of the 2000-acre Torrey Pines State Natural Reserve. Environmentally protected for 150 years, it is comprised of long stretches of sandy beaches, miles of trails leading to breathtaking views, and a lagoon inhabited by numerous species of birds and fish.

Torrey Pines Moonrise at Sunset

LA JOLLA (pages 34 – 35)

A full moon rises over the tranquil Torrey Pines State Natural Reserve. This stunning stretch of San Diego coastline is home to the rare and graceful pine variety *Pinus torreyana* that grows among the sandstone. Scenic overlooks can be reached while hiking throughout the reserve's 8 miles of meandering trails.

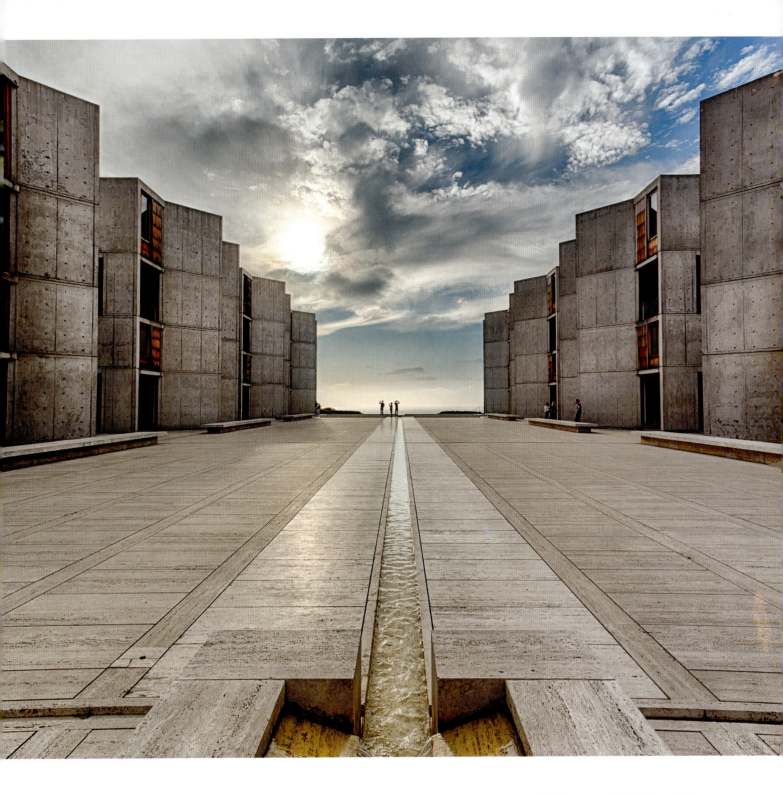

Beach Gems
(opposite, top)

Some of nature's most dynamic designs can be found in the smallest places. While kelp and seafoam may generally go unnoticed by barefoot beachgoers, here, the discerning eye of our artful photographer captures a wondrous shoreline composition of vibrant color that dances among an array of textures.

Artful Pines
(opposite, bottom)

Nestled within a burst of pine needles is a cone of the *Pinus torreyana*, the country's most rare pine species. Exclusive to San Diego County (and also found on the neighboring Channel Islands), the Torrey Pine grows in the sandy strip of coastal woodland that now includes nearly 3000 of the endangered trees.

Salk Institute for Biological Sciences
LA JOLLA *(above)*

Founded in the 1960s by Jonas Salk, M.D., developer of the polio vaccine, the Salk Institute is dedicated to the treatment and cure of diseases. Mirrored, six-story structures, designed by renowned architect Louis Kahn, create an inspirational oceanfront atmosphere for the institute's research scientists.

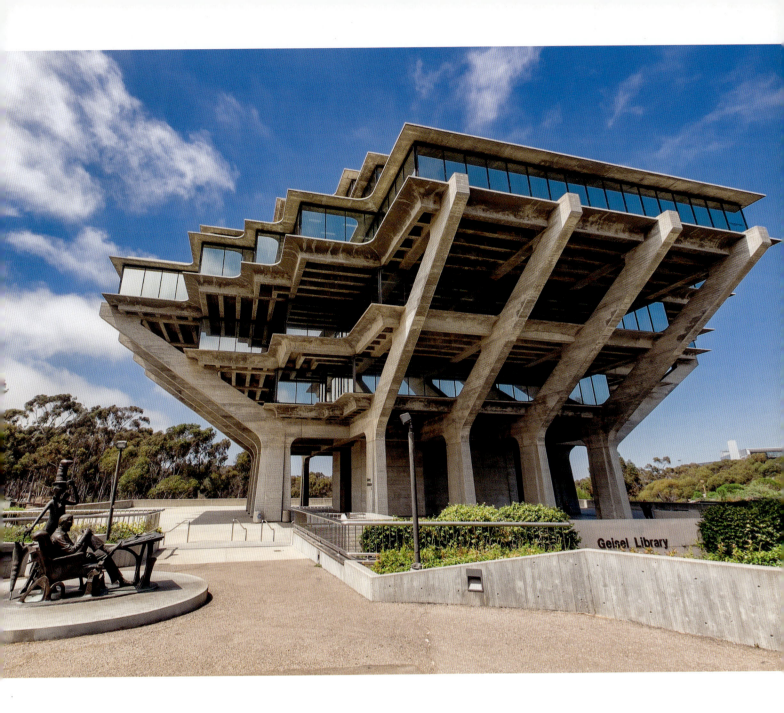

Jacobs Hall
UNIVERSITY OF CALIFORNIA *(opposite)*

A small house performs a balancing act from the rooftop of the seven-story-tall Jacobs School of Engineering. Korean artist Do Ho Suh created the eye-catching piece called *Fallen Star* as a statement of cultural displacement. Surprisingly, the house is fully-furnished and includes a lovely landscaped roof garden.

Geisel Library
UNIVERSITY OF CALIFORNIA *(above)*

Named for La Jolla residents, Audrey and Theodor Seuss Geisel (also known as Dr. Suess) the UC at San Diego Library houses an archive of 8,500 items, including sketches and manuscripts, of the famous children's book author. It also contains materials in the areas of Arts, Engineering, Social Sciences and more.

University of San Diego
UNIVERSITY CITY *(above)*

Founded in 1949, the University of San Diego is a Catholic liberal arts college located on a beautiful 180-acre campus. It merged with The College for Men and the School of Law in 1972 to become the existing university offering bachelor's, masters, and doctoral programs.

San Diego Golden Triangle
LA JOLLA *(right)*

A bustling area of business offices, high-tech industries, shopping venues, restaurants and more, the Golden Triangle encompasses an area within freeways 5, 52, and 805, and includes University Towne Center and University City.

Birch Aquarium
UNIVERSITY OF CALIFORNIA *(opposite)*

Part of the Scripps Institution of Oceanography at UC San Diego, Birch Aquarium educates the public on species found all along the California coastline. Their exhibits have been enlightening ocean-life enthusiasts since 1905.

University Towne Center
UNIVERSITY CITY

This stunning, glass-covered building is part of University Towne Center, in San Diego's Golden Triangle. UTC includes business offices along with an upscale outdoor mall complete with fitness center and a food court boasting views that overlook the UTC Ice Sports Center's ice-skating rink below.

San Diego California Temple
UNIVERSITY CITY

With its towering spires and illuminated, marble-chipped exterior, the stunning temple of The Church of Jesus Christ of Latter-day Saints is a noted San Diego landmark. The Mormon temple rests on 7.2 acres and has a total floor area of 72,000 square feet. Dedicated in 1993, it is the third temple built in California.

Congregation Beth Israel
UNIVERSITY CITY GOLDEN TRIANGLE

Dating back to 1861, Congregation Beth Israel has occupied three separate locations over a span of 150 years. It is San Diego's oldest Jewish congregation. With acclaimed architecture reminiscent of Jerusalem, the congregation's permanent home includes five buildings on three acres.

Mission Basilica San Diego de Alcalá
MISSION VALLEY *(above)*

The first of California's 21 Missions, San Diego de Alcalá was founded in 1769 by Father Junipero Serra and remains an active Catholic parish today. Historically, its massive bells were rung as a reminder of dinner or prayer time. Today, one bell rings twice per day, and all bells chime once per year on the mission's anniversary.

Interior Mission Basilica San Diego de Alcalá
MISSION VALLEY *(right)*

Named for Spanish Saint Didacus of Alcala, the Basilica's interior boasts its colorful Spanish influence. Abandoned and left in ruins until the late 1800s, it was rebuilt in 1931 after architects J. E. Loveless and J. Marshall Miller extensively researched the Mission's original details.

Scripps Pier
LA JOLLA *(opposite)*

The 1,090-foot span of Scripps Pier is captured from a mesmerizing perspective—its massive concrete piles lapped by the constant surf. The original pier was built in 1915 and rebuilt in 1988 by the Scripps Institute of Oceanography. Not a public pier, it is used exclusively for oceanographic research.

Sunset at Scripps Pier
LA JOLLA *(top)*

The sun sets over Scripps Pier, one of the largest research piers in the world. In the evening, the pier is illuminated and can be seen from a great distance. The pier and its surrounding waters are part of La Jolla Underwater Park—a 6,000-acre area dedicated to the preservation and research of marine life.

La Jolla Sunset
LA JOLLA *(bottom)*

Although its name's origin has been disputed, many agree that La Jolla was derived from the Spanish word "la joya" which quite fittingly means "the jewel." An affluent community surrounded by cliffs and beautiful beaches, La Jolla's natural beauty is apparent all along its 7-mile coastline.

Children's Pool
LA JOLLA *(above)*

Built in 1932, the seawall sheltering the Children's Pool is a choice spot for viewing harbor seals and sea lions. While the sheltered beach makes for safer conditions for human tykes, seals controversially share the area for the same reasons.

Perched
LA JOLLA *(left)*

A California brown pelican sits on his rocky perch, boasting his signature red throat pouch—prominent during mating season. Once endangered, the brown pelican's rejuvenated population is now a common coastal spectacle.

La Jolla Cove
LA JOLLA *(opposite)*

Brandts' cormorants rest from a seemingly precarious vantage point, high above the crashing surf of La Jolla Cove. The cove's small, protected beach is popular with snorkelers and kayakers. Its stunning scenic beauty make this one of San Diego's most photographed locals.

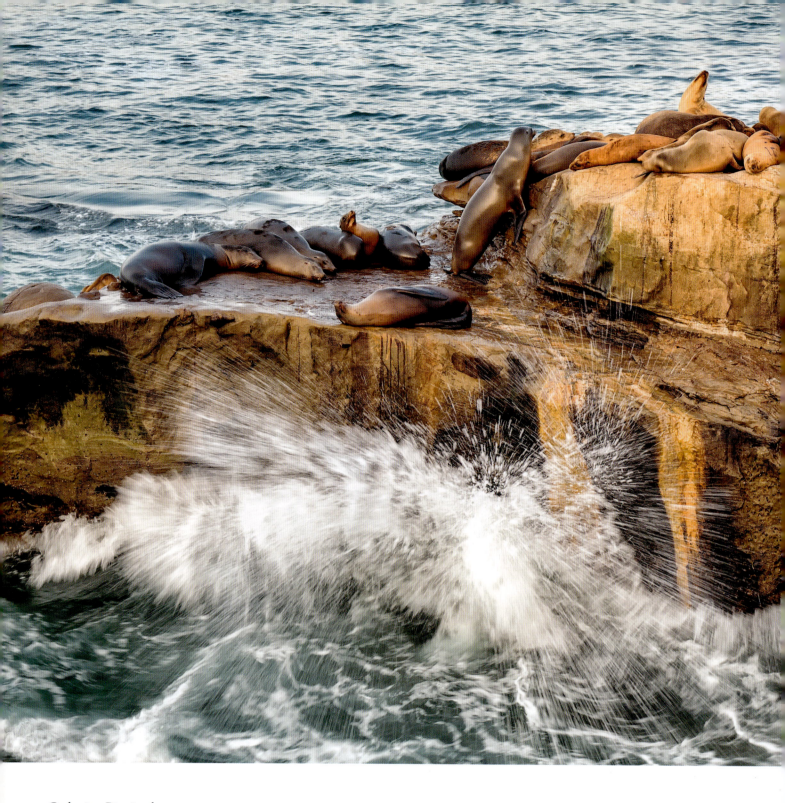

Gathering Pinnipeds
LA JOLLA

Sea lions take up residence on a comfortable, multi-tiered rock on the La Jolla coast. These playful, yet rather noisy, mammals are often found in groups, communicating in loud barks. They will feed on an array of readily available sealife including squid, and mackerel.

Perfect Landing
LA JOLLA *(top)*

Delisted as an endangered species in 2009, the *Pelecanus occidentalis*, or brown pelican, thrives along the San Diego coast. Avid fishermen, they can forcefully plunge for their dinner from heights of up to 60 feet. They lay claim to the largest pouch of all birds and, fully grown, can eat up to four pounds of fish daily.

Sea Lions
LA JOLLA *(bottom)*

Protected under the Marine Mammal Protection Act, sea lions are a common sight and can be found basking in the afternoon sun or swimming in and around the caves of La Jolla. Sea lions can be identified by their external ear flaps, a characterization not shared by their seal cousins.

La Valencia Hotel
LA JOLLA (top)

Known as La Jolla's "Pink Lady," La Valencia Hotel, designed by local architect, Reginald Johnson, first opened in 1926. With its old-world charm, stunning sea-side location, and award-winning restaurants, the 112-room hotel is an elegant retreat for Hollywood stars and travelers who prefer timeless luxury.

July 4th Celebration
LA JOLLA (bottom)

La Jollans gather at Ellen Browning Scripps Park and stake a claim for the perfect spot to celebrate the nation's birthday. The annual La Jolla Cove 4th of July celebration is a much-anticipated summer tradition where locals and visitors enjoy great food, music, and a fabulous fireworks display.

La Jolla Cove Beach

LA JOLLA

La Jolla Cove Beach is a small strip of sand flanked by sandstone cliffs. Visitors, drawn to its scenic beauty, have made this small beach one of the most photographed in the area. The beach is part of La Jolla Underwater Park Ecological Reserve which protects and preserves La Jolla's precious coastal environment.

Shops at the Cove
LA JOLLA *(above and left)*

From high-end boutiques to specialty shops, strolling La Jolla is a window shopper's paradise. Steps from the ocean, visitors enjoy shops, cafés, fine restaurants, art galleries, night clubs, and more.

Mt. Soledad Veterans Memorial
LA JOLLA *(opposite, top)*

At Mt. Soledad's 824-foot summit, this scenic memorial honors veterans from the Revolutionary War to present—both living and deceased. With plans to accommodate more, the Memorial Walls honor 3,300 vets, each with a plaque displaying their image and summary of service.

Museum of Contemporary Art
LA JOLLA *(opposite, bottom)*

Located on nearly three oceanfront acres, the Museum of Contemporary Art San Diego features large, light-filled galleries that include over 4,000 works produced since 1950. The museum features national and international artists and has expanded to a second location in downtown San Diego.

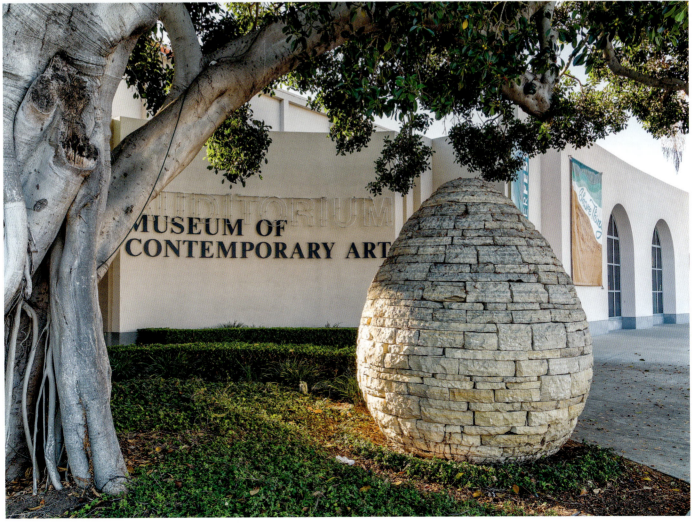

Windansea Beach
LA JOLLA

Swirling, windswept Windansea Beach is a secluded rocky beach that entices expert surfers with extreme wave action brought on by underwater reefs and a steeply sloped ocean floor. Located on Nautilus Street, the beach also features the Surf Shack—a palm-covered shack, built in 1946, now a historical landmark.

Tourmaline Surf Park Beach
PACIFIC BEACH

With dramatic cliffs reaching upwards of 75 feet, Tourmaline Surf Park Beach is one of San Diego's premier surf and sailboard locals. The park features a memorial of well-known past and present surfers—its motto reads "Surf Well, Spread Aloha, Share Waves Without Judgment."

Crystal Pier
PACIFIC BEACH *(above)*

Opened in 1927, historic Crystal Pier is a popular vacation spot that features quaint seaside cottages with plenty of shops and restaurants nearby. The 872-foot-long wooden pier is well known for fishing as well as for its spectacular panoramic ocean views.

Crystal Pier Hotel Cottages
PACIFIC BEACH *(left)*

The grand arched entry of Crystal Pier Hotel leads to charming blue and white, 1930s-style cottages where vacationers sleep to the rhythm of the waves just beneath them. High in demand during season, the one- and two-bedroom cottages are reserved at least 6 months in advance.

Mission Bay
PACIFIC BEACH

Whether paddle boarding on the bay, or surfing on the ocean, Mission Bay's 27 miles of sandy shoreline is a water sports paradise. The nation's largest man-made aquatic park, Mission Bay Park is 4,200 acres of land and water activity including moonlit cruises, sailing, jet skiing, sportfishing, beach volleyball, and more.

San Diego Crew Classic
MISSION BAY *(top and bottom)*

Organized rowing in San Diego dates back to 1888. Since then, the beloved tradition has evolved to include the largest regatta in the world. The San Diego Crew Classic draws more than 4,000 athletes to compete in nearly 100 races of varying classes. It's an exciting two-day event enjoyed by thousands of spectators.

Mission Bay Yacht Club

MISSION BAY *(above and right)*

Sailboats perform a dance of wind and water on Mission Bay. Devoted to the sport of sailing since 1943, the Mission Bay Yacht Club is an organization steeped in tradition. The club operates a Junior Sailing Program and hosts national and world championship regattas, as well as social events throughout the year.

Fiesta Island
MISSION BAY *(above)*

This spacious peninsular park in Mission Bay is popular for hiking, biking, and water sports of every kind—there's even a great off-leash dog park. The island is home to the San Diego Youth Aquatic Center which offers a summer youth camp, year-round water sports activities, as well as a venue for special events.

University of San Diego
MISSION BAY *(left)*

The glistening structure that commands the hilltop skyline is the Joan B. Kroc Institute for Peace & Justice at the University of San Diego. Seen from Fiesta Island, the renowned center for conflict resolution and human rights is also home to the university's history, political science, and international relations departments.

Belmont Park
MISSION BEACH *(above)*

This historic, seaside amusement park was initially founded in 1925 to stimulate the local economy and would eventually fall into disrepair. Today, with the restoration of both main attractions: The Plunge—a 12,000-square-foot pool—and the Giant Dipper roller coaster, Belmont Park remains as popular as ever.

Bicycling on the Boardwalk
MISSION BEACH *(right)*

The 3.5-mile Mission Beach Boardwalk is perfect for a leisurely bike ride, jog, walk, or for just kicking back to enjoy the sea breezes while people watching. Also known as Oceanfront Boardwalk, the scenic stretch has an energetic vibe with ocean views from North Pacific Beach to South Mission Beach.

SeaWorld®

MISSION BAY *(top and bottom)*

Take a thrilling waterpark ride, interact with dolphins and rays, and enjoy many of the outstanding animal attractions and environmental exhibits at SeaWorld San Diego. Located on Mission Bay, Sea-World has been offering a unique learning experience that's packed with fun for over half a century.

Turtle Reef at SeaWorld®
MISSION BAY

Curious children are held spellbound at the undersea wonders of the Turtle Reef exhibit at SeaWorld San Diego. This is truly an up-close and personal look into the magical world of nature's large, yet graceful, sea creatures and the environment in which they thrive.

Sunset Cliffs Natural Park
OCEAN BEACH *(above and opposite, bottom)*

The Native American Kumeyaay tribesmen came to this beautiful area for its abundance of sustenance from the sea and surrounding lands, and to, no doubt, bask in its extraordinary beauty. Sunset Cliffs Natural Park, along Point Loma's western shoreline, stretches 1.5 miles and covers 68 acres.

Surf's Up
OCEAN BEACH *(opposite, top)*

Surfers dot the rolling seascape in anticipation of the perfect wave. With many surfer-themed shops and pubs, along with its laid-back feel, the Ocean Beach community is a mecca for wave-riding enthusiats. It is also home to Ocean Beach Pier, which at 1,971 feet, is the longest concrete pier on the West Coast.

Sunset Cliffs Natural Park
OCEAN BEACH *(pages 68 – 69)*

Massive sandstone cliffs, carved through the ages by wind and water, provide a stunning vantage point from which to view the setting sun, and perhaps catch sight of a migrating California gray whale. The park, dedicated in 1983, includes an 18-acre linear section and 50-acre hillside section.

San Diego State University
MID CITY / COLLEGE AREA

Founded in 1897, San Diego State University is the oldest higher-learning facility in the region, and with a student body of more than 35,000, it's also the largest. Highly focused on academic excellence, it offers students 91 undergraduate majors, 78 masters, and 22 doctoral degree programs.

San Diego State University
MID CITY / COLLEGE AREA

The Conrad Prebys Aztec Student Union is home away from home for many SDSU students. Inside its classic Mission-revival design is 206,000 square feet of dining, shops, student offices, a bowling alley, and more. To the region's advantage, fifty percent of SDSU graduates remain in the San Diego area.

Junipero Serra Museum
PRESIDIO PARK

One of San Diego's most recognized landmarks, this Mission-style building marks the spot where Spanish Franciscan missionary, Father Junípero Serra founded California's first mission in 1769. Located in Presidio Park, the museum is open for tours and is available for weddings and special events.

Flower Boxes in Mission Hills
MISSION HILLS *(top)*

Planned by J.C. Nichols in the early 1900s, Mission Hills is a beautiful garden-like neighborhood, with fountains and centuries-old statues throughout the area. From bungalows to Spanish-revival style, many homes built during the early 20th century include intricate architectural details that are lovingly preserved.

Celebrating Mexican Heritage
OLD TOWN *(bottom)*

With such close proximity to the Mexican border, San Diegans have a much more natural inclination to celebrate Cinco de Mayo with fervor. At Fiesta de Reyes, the celebration seems to be an ongoing affair, with strolling Mariachi bands, colorful dancers, and, of course, exquisite Mexican fare.

Heritage Park
OLD TOWN

Colorful and beautifully restored, Heritage Park is dedicated to historic Victorian architecture. The 7.8-acre park includes seven fine structures of late 19th-century styles, such as Italianate, Stick-Eastlake, Queen Anne, and Classic Revival. As well, Temple Beth Israel, San Diego's first synagogue, can be found here.

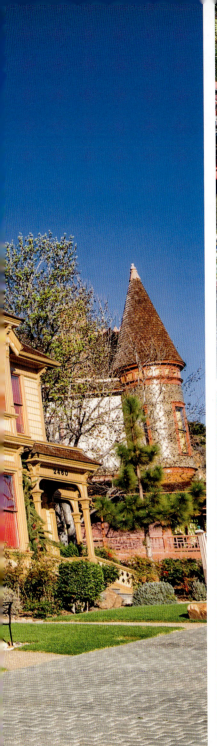

Old Town Market

OLD TOWN *(top and bottom)*

Overflowing with shops, museums, and eateries, Old Town Market is a perfect blend of history and fun. Browse through over 40 shops displaying crafts handmade by Mexican artisans, tour the haunted Whaling House, hear tales of the first settlers from storytellers, and enjoy authentic Mexican cuisine.

St. Patrick's Day Parade
BALBOA PARK *(above and left)*

Marching bagpipe bands, floats, and even Harley-riding, Irish-loving canines are among over 100 entries that take part in the San Diego St. Patrick's Day Parade and Irish Festival. The festival, held at Balboa Park, is a big part of the celebration with food, drink, crafts, and live entertainment on two stages.

Bankers Hill
MIDTOWN

Boasting stunning details, this gorgeous Victorian home is located in the Bankers Hill neighborhood of San Diego. Named for its grand homes and distinguished residents, Bankers Hill was developed during the 1890s. Walking tours offer visitors a glimpse of an array of architectural styles as well as historic sites.

Spreckels Organ Pavilion
BALBOA PARK *(above)*

A highlight of the 1915 Panama-California Exposition, the Spreckels Organ is one of the largest outdoor pipe organs in the world. It was gifted to the city in 1914 by John and Adolph Spreckels, sons of a sugar magnate. Free concerts are performed every Sunday.

View From Cabrillo Bridge
BALBOA PARK *(left)*

The lively pulse of a San Diego night is evident from the Cabrillo Bridge—a 100-year-old historic landmark. As the lights of the skyline twinkle invitingly, traffic meanders in glowing trails to and from the city.

Crescent Moon Rising
BALBOA PARK *(opposite)*

The moon rises over the illuminated tower and dome of the California Building in Balboa Park, home of San Diego Museum of Man. Designed by architect Bertram Goodhue, it was built for the 1915 Panama-California Exposition.

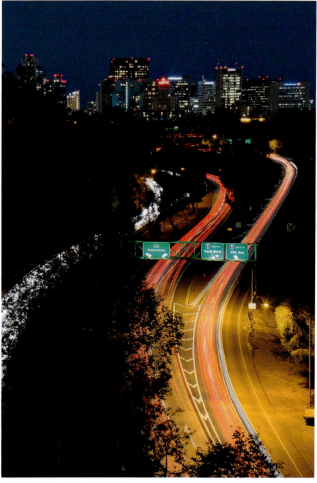

San Diego Museum of Art
BALBOA PARK

Located in Balboa Park, the city's largest and oldest art museum, the San Diego Museum of Art houses an extensive permanent collection of European, Asian, and American art. It also hosts world-renown traveling exhibits, and provides an array of educational programs, as well as lectures, films, and music.

San Diego Museum of Art
BALBOA PARK (above)

The exterior of the San Diego Museum of Art features ornate detailing that originated with the 1915 Panama-California Exposition. Chris Mueller, an architectural sculptor, oversaw the details of many of the exposition buildings. Here, the architect features life-sized likenesses of the masters Velázquez, Murillo, and Zurbarán.

San Diego Museum of Man
BALBOA PARK (right)

Among the historical figures featured on the exterior façade of the California Building is Juan Rodriguez Cabrillo, the Portuguese explorer who arrived in San Diego Bay in 1542. The figures were carved for the 1915 Panama-California Exposition by the Piccirilli Brothers, a family of talented marble sculptors.

Museum of Photographic Arts
BALBOA PARK

The Casa de Balboa building in Balboa Park houses the Model Railroad Museum, the San Diego History Center, and the Museum of Photographic Arts. MOPA's photography collection is nothing short of inspirational. The museum also hosts lectures, workshops, film screenings, and special events.

California Building Dome
BALBOA PARK *(above)*

With a deep San Diego sky as a backdrop, colorful tiles of blue, yellow, black, and green adorn the dome of the California Building in Balboa Park. Etched into the dome is a biblical inscription that translates, "A land of wheat, and barley, and vines, and fig-trees, and pomegranates; a land of olive oil, and honey."

San Diego Museum of Man
BALBOA PARK *(right)*

The 198-foot-tall tower of the California Building is one of the city's most recognizable landmarks. The building houses the Museum of Man, a museum whose anthropological roots originated from the 1915 Panama-California Exhibition's exhibit called "The Story of Man through the Ages."

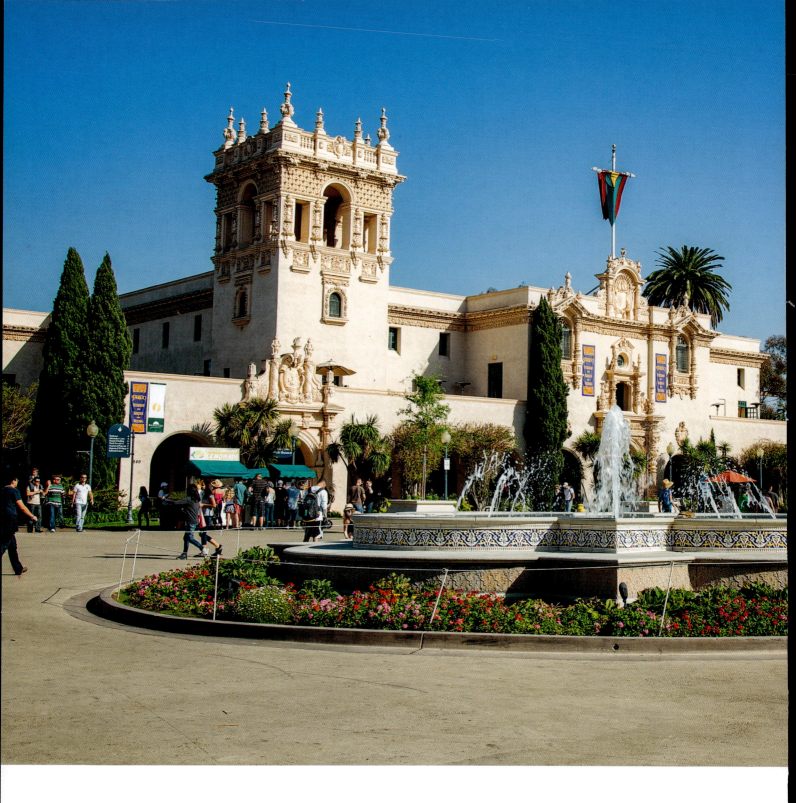

House of Hospitality
BALBOA PARK

The Balboa Park Visitors Center is appropriately located in the House of Hospitality Building. Stocked with maps, brochures, and souvenirs, it's a great starting point for vacationers taking part in all the park has to offer. After a day of sight-seeing, enjoy dinner at The Prado, an award-winning restaurant located here.

Natural History Museum

BALBOA PARK (top)

From the gilded kings of ancient Egypt to the fossilized remains of Southern California's prehistoric residents, to understanding our environment today, theNAT educates and inspires. TheNAT, along with 26 other art, culture, and science institutions in the park, is a member of the Balboa Park Cultural Partnership.

Spanish Village Art Center

BALBOA PARK (bottom)

Art lovers flock to the Spanish Village Art Center to see paintings and handmade crafts of over 200 artisans. Over 30 studios and galleries can be found among the village's charming buildings and courtyards that were built in Balboa Park for the California Pacific International Exposition in 1935.

Marston House Museum & Gardens
BALBOA PARK (top)

Designed in 1905 by internationally renowned architects William Sterling Hebbard and Irving Gill, the Marston House was built for noted civic leader, George W. Marston and his wife, Anna. The meticulous 8,500 square-foot home and garden was gifted to the city in 1987 and is since open to the public.

San Diego Lawn Bowling Club
BALBOA PARK (bottom)

"Bowls" or "Lawn Bowls" is a centuries-old game that is still played at the lawn bowling greens in Balboa Park. With over 100 members, the Lawn Bowling Club, founded in 1932, hosts a number of tournaments, and offers group bowling events for parties and corporate outings, as well as free lessons.

Alcazar Garden
BALBOA PARK (opposite)

The Alcazar Garden, in Balboa Park, displays 7,000 colorful annuals, season to season. Visitors can sit beneath a shady pergola and admire the garden's embellished fountains and beautiful flowers that are surrounded by finely trimmed box hedges. The garden is modeled after those of Alcazar Castle in Seville, Spain.

Japanese Friendship Garden
BALBOA PARK *(above and left)*

With its koi pond, ornamental trees, and stone arrangements, the garden is an experience that delights all of the senses. It is a blooming declaration of the friendly bond between San Diego and her sister city, Yokohama. The garden also includes an exhibition hall and offers workshops and horticultural classes.

Botanical Building and Lily Pond
BALBOA PARK *(top and bottom)*

An inspiration for photographers and painters alike, the serene Lily Pond in front of the Bontanical Building, provides a peaceful haven for visitors of Balboa Park. Envisioned by Alfred Robinson for the 1915 Panama-California Exposition, the enormous lath structure is one of the largest of its kind in the world.

Stop and Smell the Roses
BALBOA PARK *(opposite)*

With over 130 varieties of roses, the Inez Grant Parker Memorial Rose Garden fills 3 acres of Balboa Park with fragrant blooms that peak in April and May. Located on the grounds near the Natural History Museum, the garden is maintained by volunteers from the Balboa Park Rose Garden Corp.

Balboa Park Golf Course
BALBOA PARK *(top)*

Even the most focused golfers would be easily distracted by the stunning vistas afforded at the Balboa Golf Course. Designed by William P. Bell, views of the city skyline, Pacific Ocean, Point Loma, and Balboa Park can be seen from challenging elevations along the 18-hole par 72 and 9-hole executive courses.

San Diego Air and Space Museum
BALBOA PARK *(bottom)*

A passenger jet soars above the San Diego Air and Space Museum where the history of flight is archived and new technologies are explored. The museum has an extensive collection of aircraft and artifacts, books and films, educational programs, as well as special exhibits for aeronautic enthusiasts of all ages.

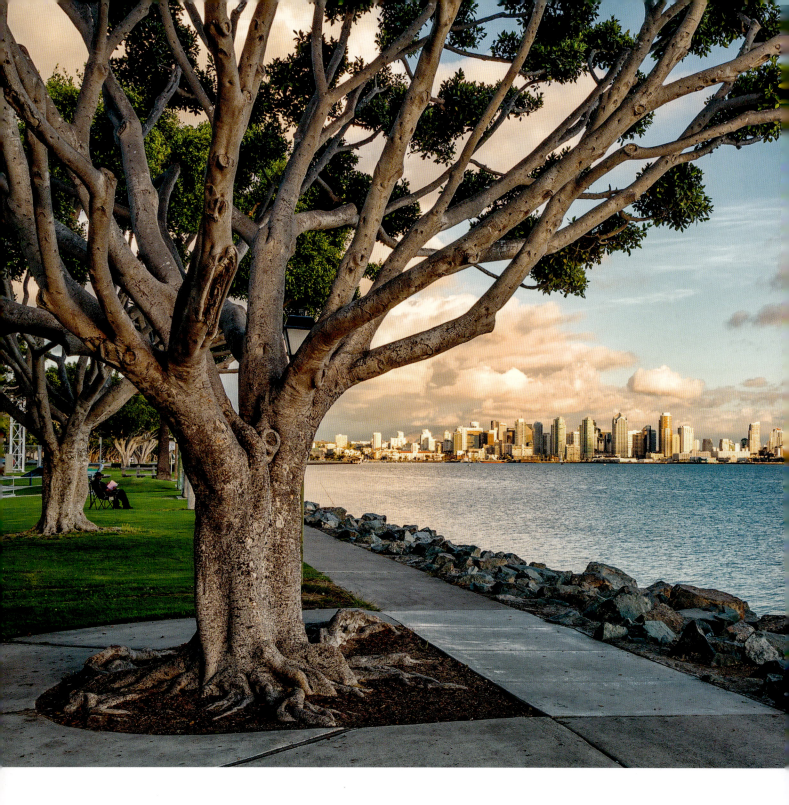

Skyline from Harbor Island
HARBOR ISLAND

Harbor Island is a 2-mile-long, man-made peninsula that provides a relaxing respite while taking in dynamic skyline views and the comings and goings on the bay. Although only a few hundred feet wide, the island includes a shoreline walking path flanked by mature shade trees and sparkling blue waters.

Harbor Drive
HARBOR ISLAND *(top)*

Sailboats rest on their moorings in the calm bay along San Diego's Harbor Drive. The busy road meanders along the city's bustling waterfront, accessing marinas, ports, waterfront parks, hotels, cruise lines, a U.S. Coast Guard Station, the shops and restaurants of Seaport Village, and more.

Skyline
HARBOR ISLAND *(bottom)*

The view of the San Diego skyline from a Hornblower cruise is a breathtaking sight, with a forest of towering buildings surrounding a crystal-blue bay. It has all the amenities of a big city, while maintaining all the charm of a small town. San Diego is a Pacific Coast gem with a laid-back feel.

Cancer Survivors Park
SPANISH LANDING *(above)*

Inspired by his own recovery, Richard Bloch and his wife, Annette, donated Cancer Survivors Park as an encouragement to others fighting the disease. The park features *Cancer...There's Hope*, a sculpture by renowned artist Victor Salmones. The piece depicts the hopeful journey from diagnosis to success.

West Basin
SPANISH LANDING *(left)*

Lined with slips harboring everything from day sailers to mega yachts, the waterfront accommodates a huge boating community. Ideal conditions and picture-perfect surroundings make cruising these waters a favorite pastime. Anglers know the West Basin to be a prime spot for fishing.

Pearl of the Pacific
SHELTER ISLAND *(above)*

Among the elements included in the Pacific Rim Park sculpture is the bubbling fountain, *Pearl of the Pacific*. Created by James Hubbell with the help of architectural students, the fountain, along with stylized Chinese fans and colorful mosaic tiles, represent San Diego's neighboring cities along the Pacific Rim.

Shelter Island
SHELTER ISLAND *(right)*

Connected to the mainland by a small causeway, Shelter Island is not an actual island. The bed of this 1.2-mile-long strip was created from the dredging of a channel entrance to San Diego Bay during the early 1930s, and, today, is home to luxurious hotels, restaurants, parks, and marinas.

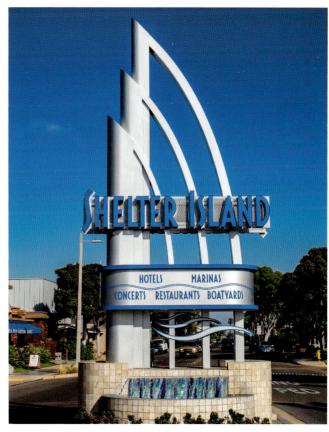

Shelter Island Marinas
SHELTER ISLAND

With its deep waters and convenient accessibility to the Pacific Ocean, the marinas on Shelter Island attract large luxurious yachts. Each September, Shelter Island hosts YachtFest, where sea-cruising enthusiasts can catch a glimpse of multi-million-dollar super yachts and daydream about lavish lifestyles.

Cabrillo Tide Pools

POINT LOMA *(above and right)*

Pools form along the rocky shores of Point Loma during low tide revealing an abundant ecosystem. Nature lovers poke and prod among a variety of brightly colored marine plants and sea creatures such as octopi, hermit crabs, urchins, snails, and more waiting to be discovered at Cabrillo National Monument.

Old Point Loma Lighthouse
POINT LOMA *(opposite, top)*

First lighted in 1855, the squat, picturesque tower evokes a by-gone era when grand sailing ships navigated San Diego Bay. One of eight lights first established along the West Coast, its usefulness was short lived because of its foggy location. Refurbished by the National Park Service, the lighthouse is open to the public.

Fort Rosecrans National Cemetery
POINT LOMA *(opposite, bottom)*

Over 86,000 grave sites line the rolling landscape of Fort Rosecrans National Cemetery. Named for Union Civil War General, William Starke Rosecrans, the site, overlooking the Pacific Ocean, also includes many monuments and memorials. The 77-acre cemetery was deemed a California Historical Landmark in 1932.

Harbor Views
POINT LOMA *(above)*

Layers of sky, clouds, and mountains are interwoven with the icons of a modern seaside metropolis in this pastel landscape display. One can only imagine the awe of Juan Rodríguez Cabrillo and the members of his expedition as they entered the bay and first landed at Point Loma in 1542.

Seaport Village
EMBARCADERO (opposite, top)

Jetskiers meander from beneath the Coronado Bridge along the waters of Embarcadero Marina Park. Embarcadero is a waterfront gem comprised of historic maritime museums, fabulous seafood restaurants and the Seaport Village experience that offers over 50 shops, eateries, and entertainment.

Hornblower Cruises
HARBOR DRIVE (opposite, bottom)

Stunning views of the San Diego skyline, along with lively coastline activity, may be best viewed from the deck of a luxurious cruise ship. Popular for weddings and special events, Hornblower Cruises launch from the Embarcadero and invite visitors to come aboard to enjoy a variety of dinner cruises and holiday excursions.

Point Loma Station Light
POINT LOMA (above)

Known as the New Point Loma Lighthouse, the historic tower was first lit in 1891. More visible than its predecessor, Old Point Loma Lighthouse, its design is the only one of its kind found on the West Coast. Automated in 1973, it has since been updated with brighter and more energy-efficient technology.

Morning
EMBARCADERO *(above, left)*

A lone gull surveys his surroundings from atop the smooth, strong lines of a 6'3" stretching granite figure in Embarcadero Marina Park near Seaport Village. *Morning*, created by the late renowned sculptor, Donal Hord, was carved from a 1.5-ton block of locally quarried black diorite.

Guardian of Water
SAN DIEGO BAY *(above, right)*

Located at the plaza of the County Administration Center, *Guardian of Water* was carved from a 22-ton granite block. Renowned artist, Donal Hord sculpted the female water bearer in his distinct style. The artist also created a replica that was presented to San Diego's sister city Yokohama, Japan.

Unconditional Surrender
SAN DIEGO BAY *(opposite)*

America's most famous kiss was photographed by Alfred Eisenstaedt and published in *Life* magazine in 1945. The legendary smooch between a sailor and a nurse during the ecstatic celebration in Times Square, marking the end of WWII, is preserved in this 25-foot-sculpture on the San Diego waterfront.

Embarcadero Marina Park
EMBARCADERO *(top)*

Gentle ocean breezes, relaxing green spaces, and mild temperatures make for a great day of kite flying at Embarcadero Marina Park. Overlooking the Coronado Bridge, the park, divided into north and south sections, is known for its scenic beauty and proximity to Seaport Village's shops, eateries, museums, and hotels.

Marriott Marquis Hotel
EMBARCADERO *(bottom)*

The gleaming exterior of the Marriott Marquis San Diego Marina is a testament to the ultimate in luxury waterfront hotels. The spectacular hotel boasts 1,360 guestrooms with sweeping views of San Diego Bay, a private marina with 446 slips, and a variety of excellent fine dining options.

Seaport Village
EMBARCADERO *(opposite)*

Opened in 1980, Seaport Village is comprised of dozens of boutiques, galleries, restaurants, and cafés, and is convenient to the towering Manchester Grand Hyatt hotel. Tourists can stroll along 4 miles of cobblestone paths in search of the perfect keepsake while enjoying spectacular bay views and vibrant sunsets.

Seaport Village
EMBARCADERO *(opposite)*

Beautiful fountains surrounded by well-manicured landscaping, along with pleasant ponds, are all part of the Seaport Village experience. Once the location of a shipyard, the 14-acre shopping mecca is a popular downtown destination for window shopping, live music, or enjoying the quarter-mile bayside boardwalk,

San Diego Convention Center
DOWNTOWN *(top and bottom)*

Built in 1989, the San Diego Convention Center boasts an area of 1.7 million square feet and comprises an exhibition hall, a stunning pavilion, spacious meeting rooms and ballrooms, as well as outdoor terraces that afford panoramic views of San Diego Bay. It is one of the largest of its kind in North America.

Central Library

DOWNTOWN *(opposite, top and bottom)*

San Diego Public Library includes 35 branch libraries as well as the striking Central Library. Recognized by its enormous dome constructed of tubular steel beams and tension cables, the new library was designed by renowned architect, Rob Quigley. Opened in 2013, the Central Library offers guided tours.

El Cortez Hotel

DOWNTOWN *(above)*

A historic landmark in downtown San Diego, the El Cortez Apartment Hotel was built in 1927. Harry Handlery purchased the hotel in 1951 and made extensive changes, including the world's first hydraulic, outdoor glass elevator. The iconic building is listed on the National Register of Historic Places.

Petco Park
DOWNTOWN *(top)*

Home of the beloved San Diego Padres, Petco Park is a state-of-the-art ballpark with a capacity of over 42,000. Opened in 2004, the $411-million-dollar park includes 5,000 club seats, 58 luxury suites, restaurants, and rooftop seating. Its brick, steel, and stucco design gives the modern structure a warm retro feel.

Harbor Drive
DOWNTOWN *(bottom)*

City lights embellish San Diego's vibrant waterfront all along Harbor Drive. Teeming with hotels, restaurants, museums, parks, marinas, and more, Harbor Drive is where visitors and locals can find some of the best of what "America's Finest City" has to offer.

Gaslamp Quarter
DOWNTOWN *(top)*

A historic district with a checkered past, San Diego's cultural hot spot, Gaslamp Quarter is the place to go for a great night out on the town. Victorian buildings against a backdrop of modern architecture, the area boasts an abundance of art galleries, night clubs, concert halls, and theaters throughout a 16.5-block area.

Little Italy
DOWNTOWN *(bottom)*

Little Italy invites all to taste the fruits of San Diego's oldest neighborhood business district. Once a major player in the tuna fishing industry, the area's history will be archived thanks to the Preserve Little Italy Initiative—a program sponsored by San Diego State University and the Little Italy Association of San Diego.

Coronado Island
CORONADO *(opposite, top)*

Brightly colored umbrellas dot the landscape of the Coronado Ferry Landing Beach. A charming and friendly city just across the bay from the city of San Diego, Coronado is often referred to as Coronado Island. However, the nearly mile-wide "island" actually sits at the end of a long, narrow peninsula.

Coronado Golf Course
CORONADO *(opposite, bottom)*

Spacious fairways with breathtaking views, along with a consistently comfortable climate, make this one of the most desirable public courses in the country. Opened in 1957, the par-72 course offers a challenging round, as well as driving range, pro shop, youth programs, lessons, and delicious fare from the Bayside Grill.

Coronado Bridge from Tidelands Park
CORONADO *(above)*

Sparkling street lights mimic a shimmering moon on a mild California evening. Connecting the city of Coronado to the mainland in a graceful 2.12-mile curve, the Coronado Bridge first opened in 1969. The 200-foot-tall structure was awarded the "Most Beautiful Bridge" in 1970 by the American Institute of Steel.

Hotel Del Coronado
CORONADO

Recognized by its distinguished Victorian charm and bright red rooftops, the "Hotel Del" first opened in 1888 and has been a major factor in Coronado's development. This National Historic Landmark has received American presidents, Hollywood stars, and notable guests such as Thomas Edison and Babe Ruth.

Hotel Del Coronado
CORONADO (above)

Spread over 28 acres of prime oceanfront, this historic landmark resort consists of the main Victorian Building, along with luxurious cottage suites and villas. Elisha Babcock and H.L. Story founded the hotel and their grandiose vision would be listed among the world's best resort hotels for the next 125 years.

Hotel Del Coronado
CORONADO (right)

Recently renovated with modern conveniences, the lobby of the Hotel Del Coronado still evokes a by-gone era. Guests will find the hotel's history to be an interesting part of their stay, from notable past guests, to the ghost of Kate Morgan, who died here in 1892 and has yet to check out.

San Diego Bay

SAN DIEGO BAY (top and bottom)

The deep turquoise waters of San Diego Bay surround a bustling oceanfront including the stunning convention center, glistening hotels, active marinas, and the historic USS *Midway* museum. To many San Diegans, this thriving waterfront is more than just miles of scenic beauty—it is a way of life.

San Diego from Coronado Island
CORONADO

The intrinsic beauty of the city skyline evokes a modern Emerald City, as seen from Coronado Island, nicknamed for the fantastical metropolis conjured from the mind of L. Frank Baum. Author of *Dorothy and the Wizard of Oz*, Baum rented a charming home here and was no doubt inspired by this enchanting island.

National Salute to Bob Hope
SAN DIEGO BAY *(top)*

With seven military bases in San Diego, the city has a proud military history. Legendary comedian, Bob Hope entertained U.S. troops at worldwide outposts for over 50 years. The sculpture *A National Salute to Bob Hope and the Military* honors the exemplary service of both Hope and U.S. servicemen and women.

Sand Sculpting Challenge
SAN DIEGO BAY *(bottom)*

Master sand sculptors from around the world gather in San Diego for the annual Sand Sculpting Challenge & 3D Art Exposition. Incredible creations, some weighing over 10 tons, are carved with amazing detail. The 4-day festival also includes artisans' hand-made crafts, live entertainment, and children's activities.

Spinnaker Sailing
SAN DIEGO BAY *(above)*

Colorful, wind-filled spinnakers make for an exhilarating sailing experience on the glistening waters of San Diego Bay where the boating lifestyle thrives. Whether a novice or an old salt, San Diego has an array of sailing options including lessons, sailing clubs, local charters, and wonderful exotic excursions.

Busker Festival
SAN DIEGO BAY *(right)*

Each year, San Diego's Seaport Village invites the world's most unique street performers—or *buskers*—to display their remarkable talents at this fun 2-day festival. Sword swallowers, human statues, fire eaters, knife jugglers, acrobatic acts, and more amuse and delight during this exclusive Southern California event.

Festival of Sail
SAN DIEGO BAY *(top and opposite)*

Majestic schooners breeze in for the West Coast's largest tall ship festival. Each year, the Maritime Museum hosts the event that begins with an awe-inspiring parade of stately vessels. Climb aboard a historic ship, feel the thrill of a reenactment of blasting cannons, and enjoy great food and fun all along the North Embarcadero.

Bill of Rights Schooner
CHULA VISTA *(bottom)*

The historic schooner, *Bill of Rights*, rests at the docks of the California Yacht Marina in Chula Vista. The 137-foot gaff-rigged schooner provides educational adventures, sunset cruises, and private charters. Affluent and diverse, Chula Vista—or *beautiful view*—is San Diego County's second largest city.

Anza-Borrego State Park
EAST COUNTY *(above and left)*

The name of the nation's largest desert park is derived from a combination of Juan Bautista de Anza, a Spanish explorer, and *borrego*, a Spanish word meaning bighorn sheep—the elusive and endangered species that live among some rocky areas of the 600,000-acre park.

Anza-Borrego Desert State Park
EAST COUNTY *(opposite)*

Geological wonders sculpted by millions of years of wind and earth movement can be found at Anza-Borrego Desert State Park. Covering one-fifth of San Diego County, it includes hundreds of miles of dirt roads and 12 wilderness areas with diverse wild flowers, reptiles, coyotes, bobcats, migrating hawks, and more.

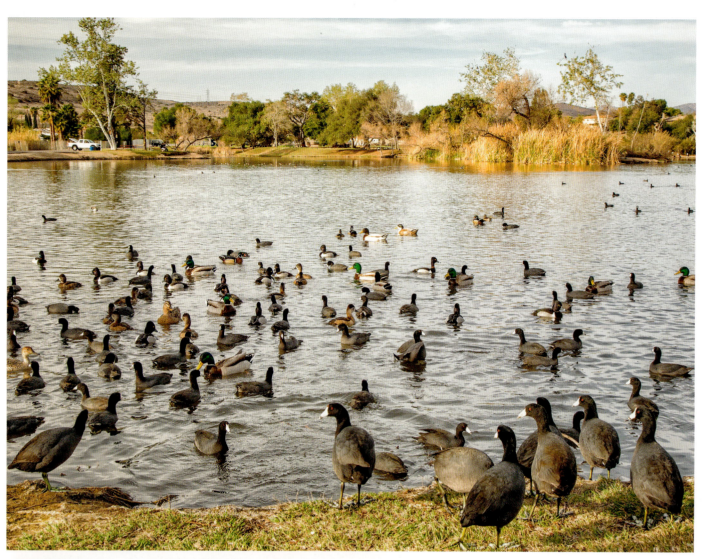

Santee Lakes Recreation Preserve
SANTEE *(above and left)*

Waterfowl gather along one of the seven scenic lakes found within the 190-acre Santee Lakes Recreation Preserve. Located just outside San Diego, Santee Lakes is an outdoor enthusiast's paradise where fishing, boating, bird watching, biking and more can be enjoyed all throughout this lakeside camping retreat.

Mission Trails Regional Park
MISSION VALLEY

Sun drenched hillsides of Mission Trails Regional Park display Mother Nature's splendor. The 5,900-acre park was established in 1974, however the Kumeyaay had made use of the land well before then. The park's Visitor Center helps nature lovers explore among the 40 miles of hiking and horseback riding trails.

Pauma Valley

EAST COUNTY *(top and bottom)*

Pauma Valley groves produce an abundance of avocados and citrus along parts of its mountainous terrain. This unincorporated area, situated at the base of the Palomar Mountains, is home to several Indian reservations, the Casino Pauma, and the residences of the Pauma Valley Country Club.

Love Valley
EAST COUNTY *(above)*

A rusty old barn sits in a meadow in Love Valley, where wide-open mountain grasslands beckon hikers to enjoy a romantic adventure. Love Valley, located within the Cleveland National Forest, is an easy 2-mile hike, with stunning views of Lake Henshaw.

Lake Henshaw Valley
EAST COUNTY *(right)*

Viewed from Mount Palomar, the sun rises above Lake Henshaw, casting the day's first warm rays over the valley. Quiet and remote, Lake Henshaw, located approximately 60 miles northeast of San Diego, is a county reservoir whose beautiful surroundings attract hikers, campers, bird watchers, and anglers.

Steve Gould has been photographing landscape, nature, wildlife and travel professionally since 2004, but his love of photography began forty years before, during a summer traveling in Europe. He was a professor of chemistry at the University of Connecticut and Oregon State University, an Executive Director at Merck Pharmaceuticals in New Jersey, and Chief Scientific Officer at Mera Pharmaceuticals in San Diego. After living on both the east and west coasts, Steve returned to California in 2002.

His photographs capture stirring vistas and ephemeral moments, presenting images that explore the shapes, textures, and colors of our magnificent world. He has continued in this vein to capture the beauty and qualities of San Diego and its surrounding communities for this new book.

Steve's photography has been featured in the San Diego Natural History Museum and the Oceanside Museum of Art, as well as in galleries in San Diego, Sedona, San Clemente, and Carlsbad. He has been a winner in Nature's Best Photography's "Ocean Views" 2012 competition and the Nature Conservancy 2013 Calendar competition. His prints are found in numerous private and corporate collections, including Kaiser Permanente (San Diego), City of Hope National Medical Center, and Scripps Institute of Oceanography.

To see more of Steve's work or to purchase photographs, including those found in this book, visit his website at www.stevegouldphotography.com.

Award-winning graphic designer, **Sara Day,** never ceases to be inspired by the beauty and unique qualities of regions throughout the United States. A native of Gloucester, Massachusetts, Sara has enjoyed a long career working with publishers, photographers, and advertising agencies. She now resides in Vero Beach, Florida where she continues to use her talents to create exquisite photo journals as well as high-end promotional materials. To see more, visit www.sypdesign.com and www.twinlightspub.com.